Bastard Secret

Hilarious Swear Word Coloring Book

For Fun & Stress Releasing

Charles C. Golden

Happy Coloring!

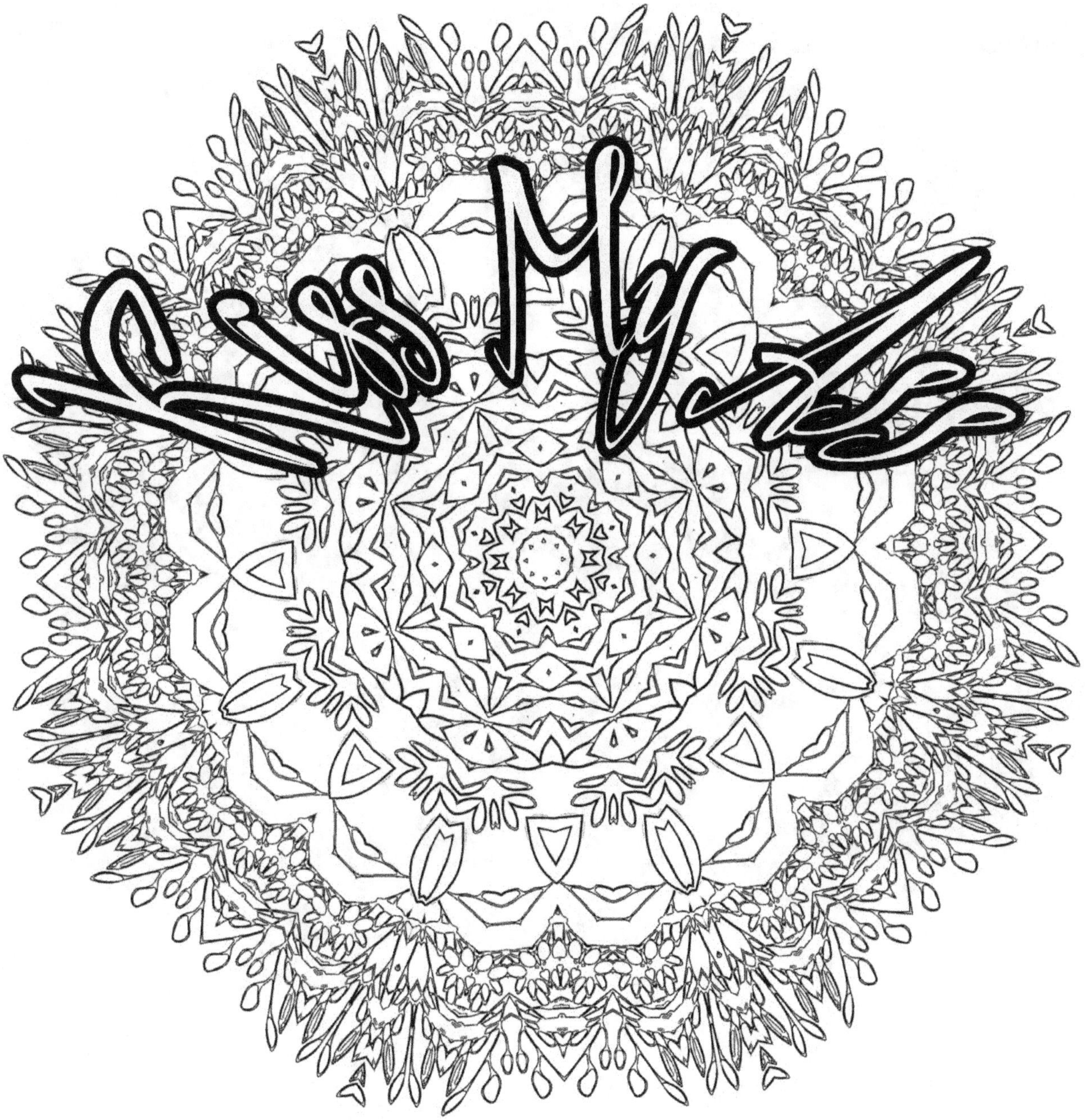
Kiss My Ass

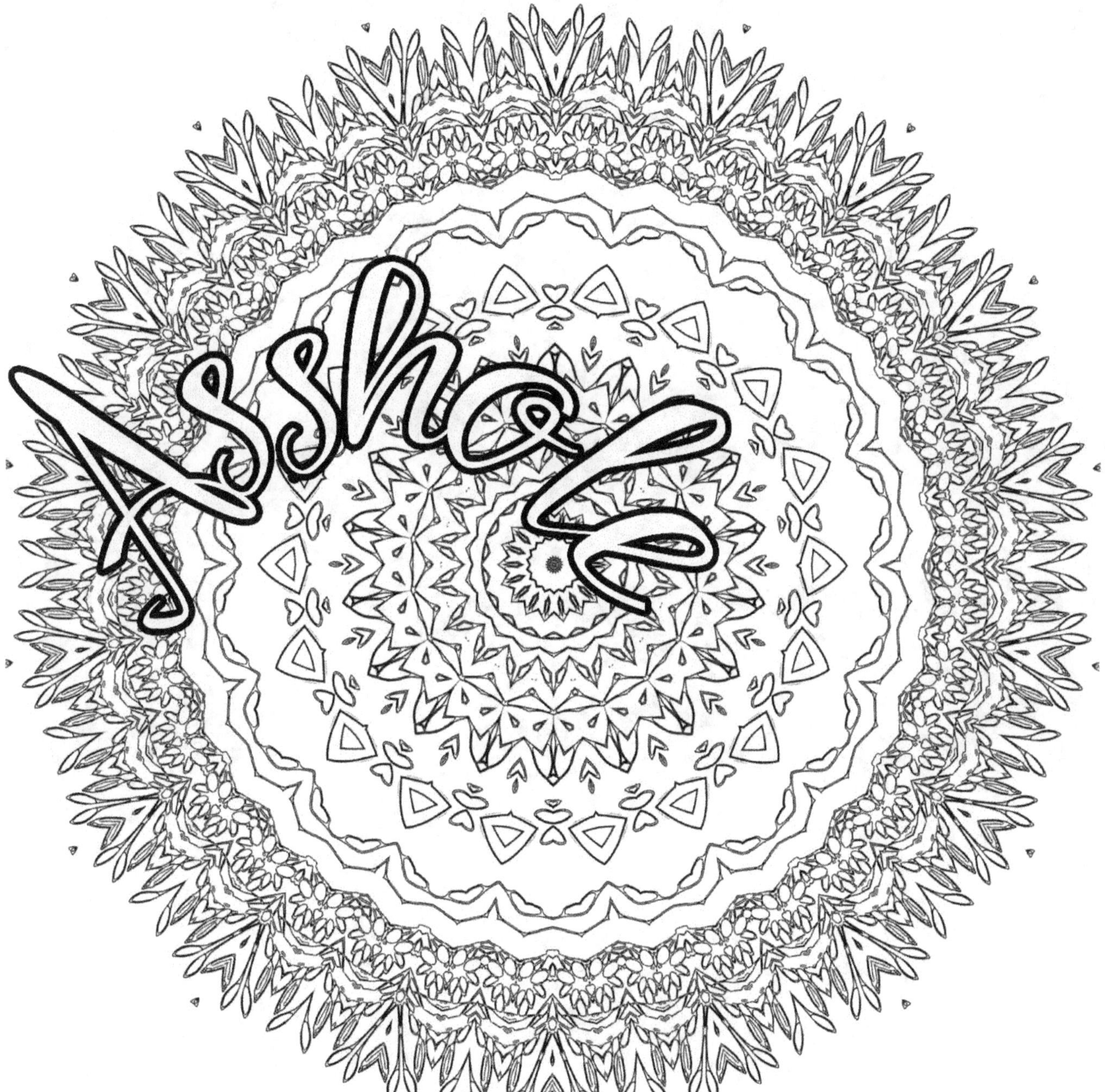
Asshole

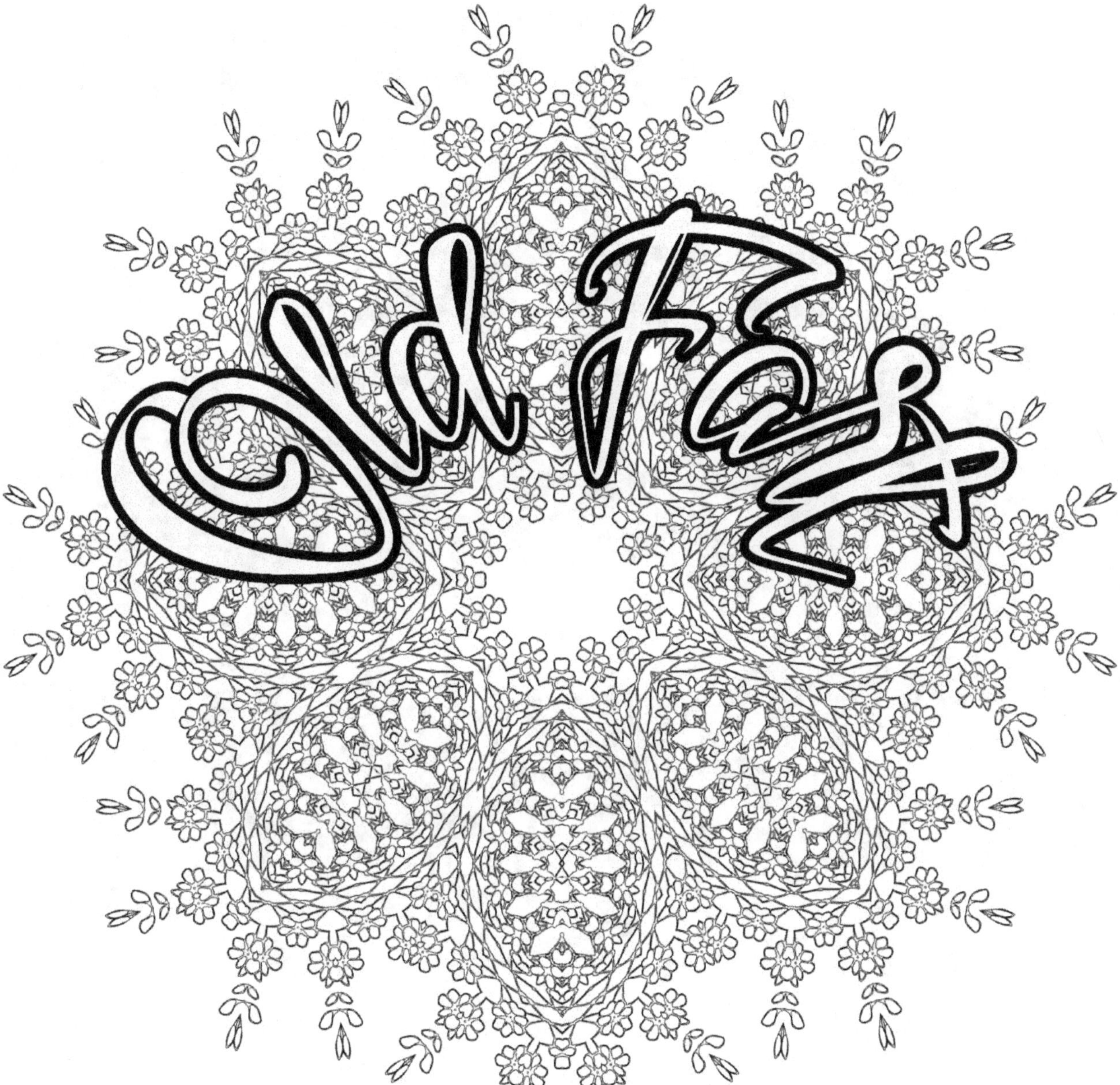
Old Fart

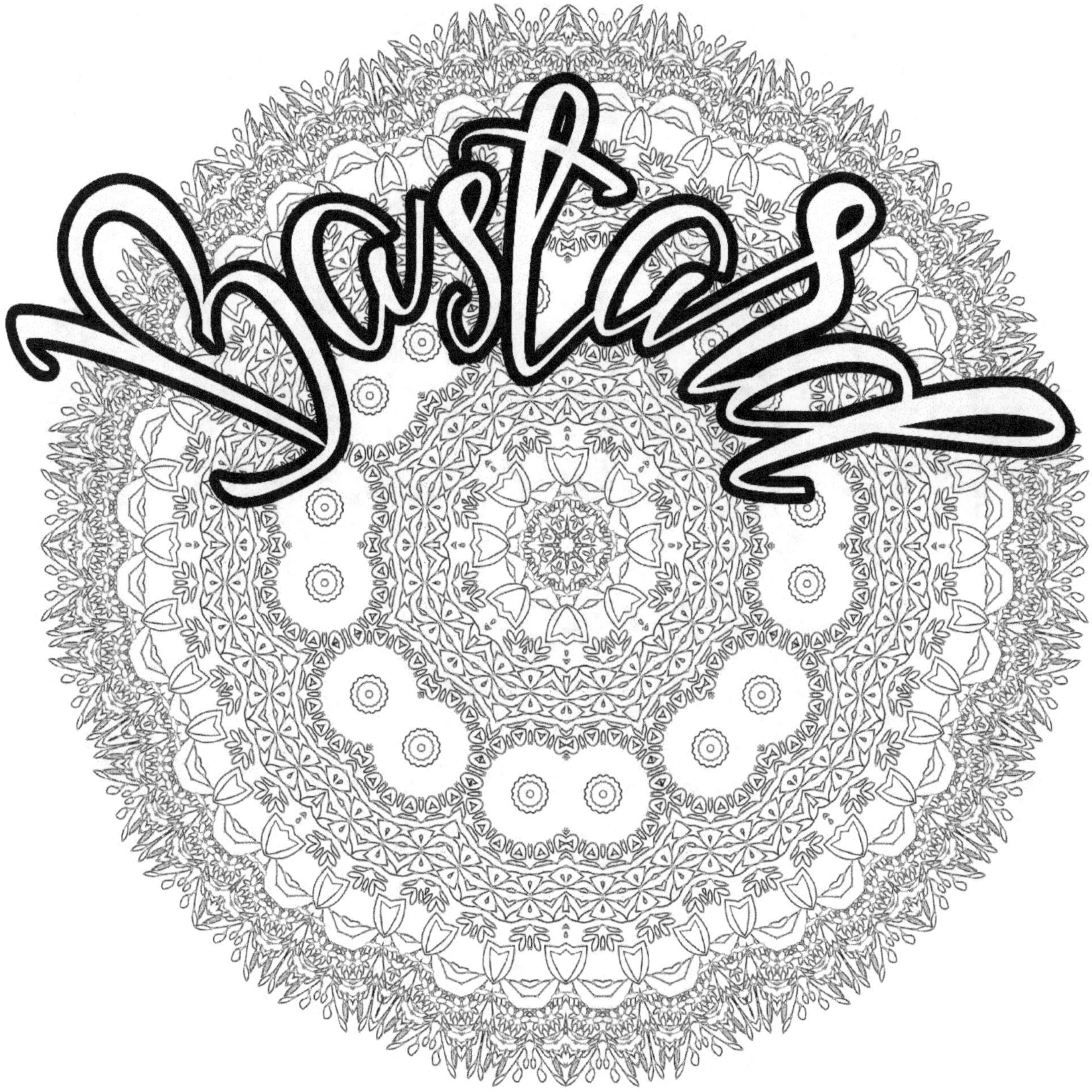
bastard

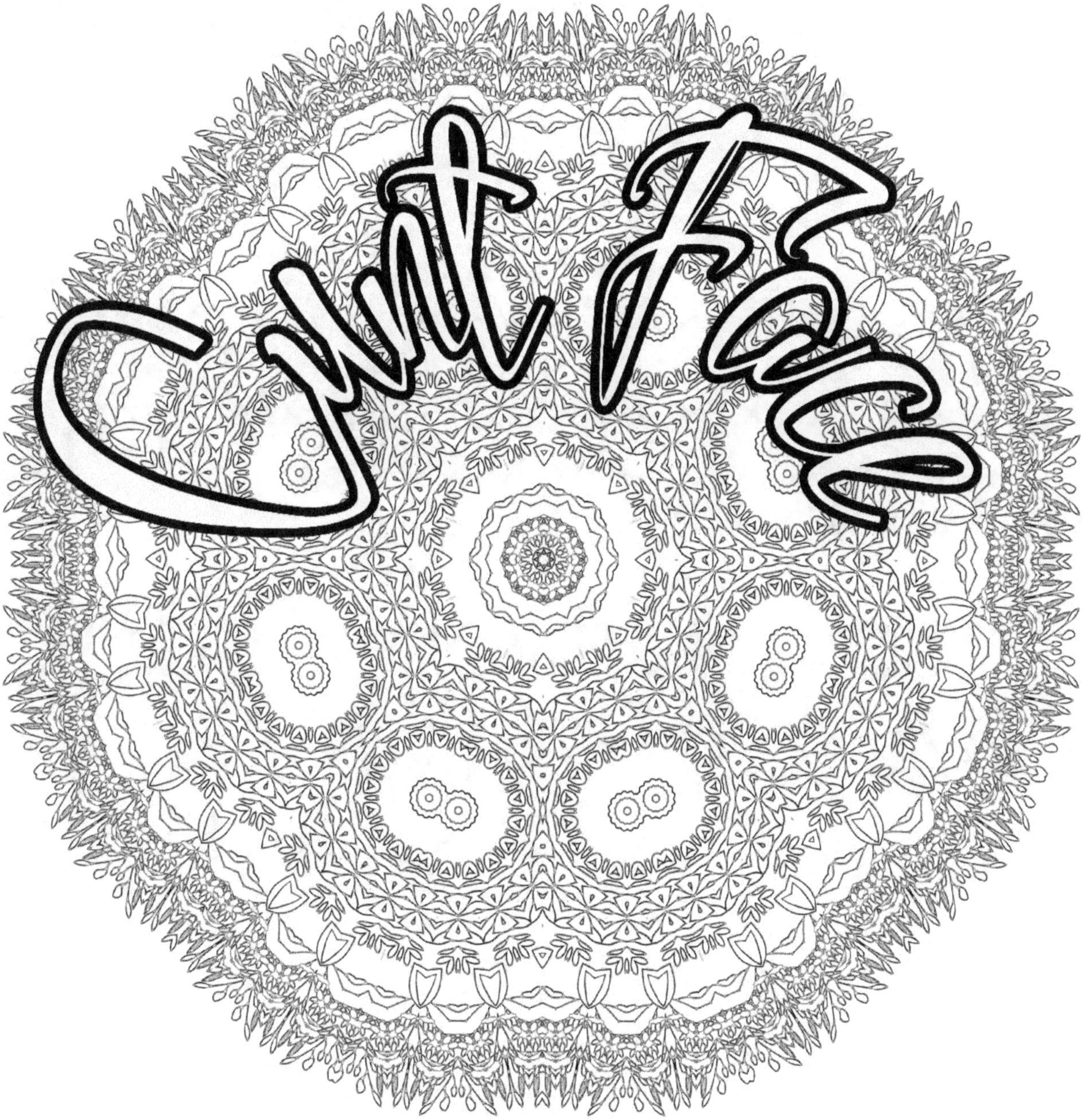
Cunt Face

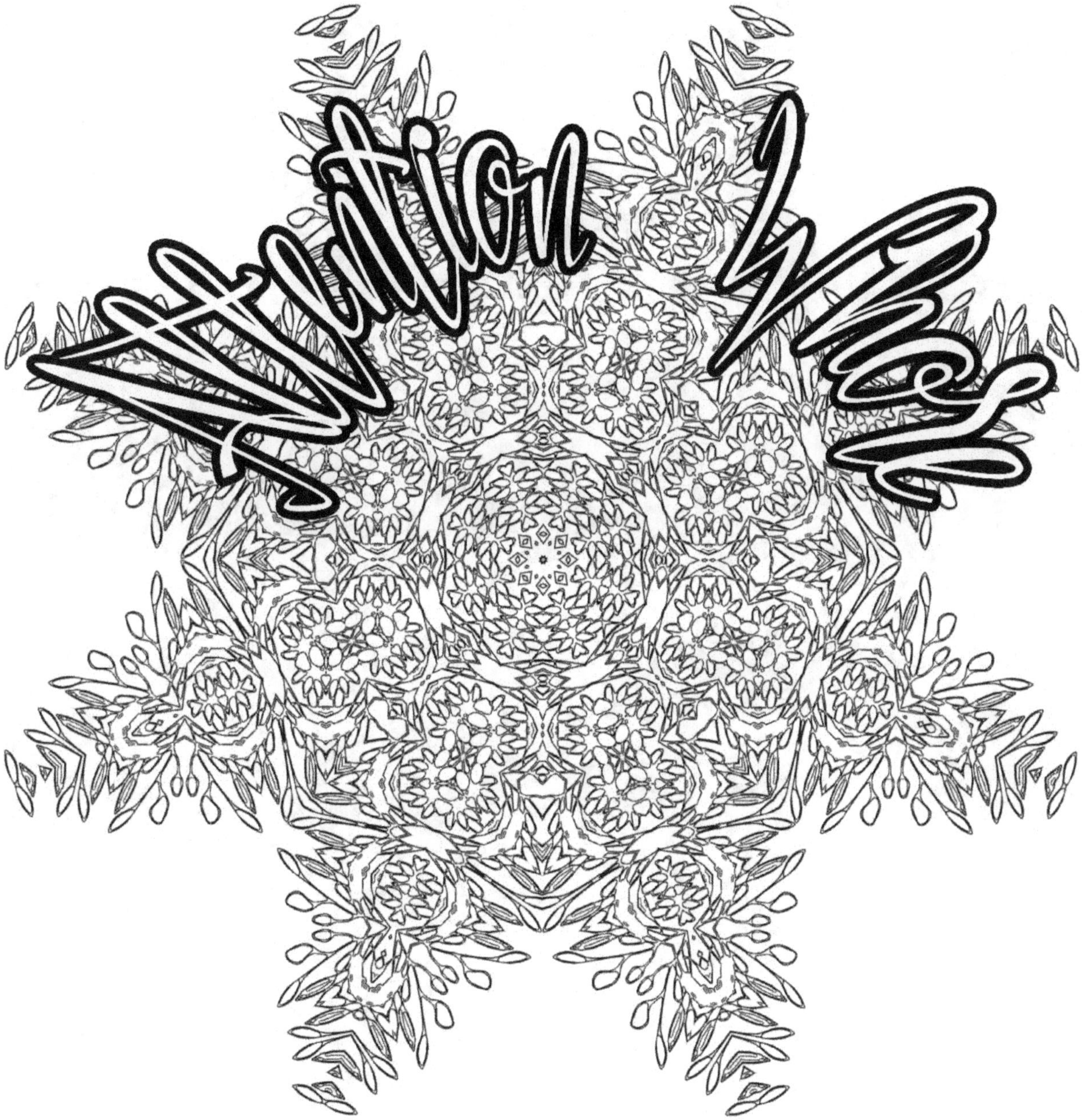
Nutrition Whey

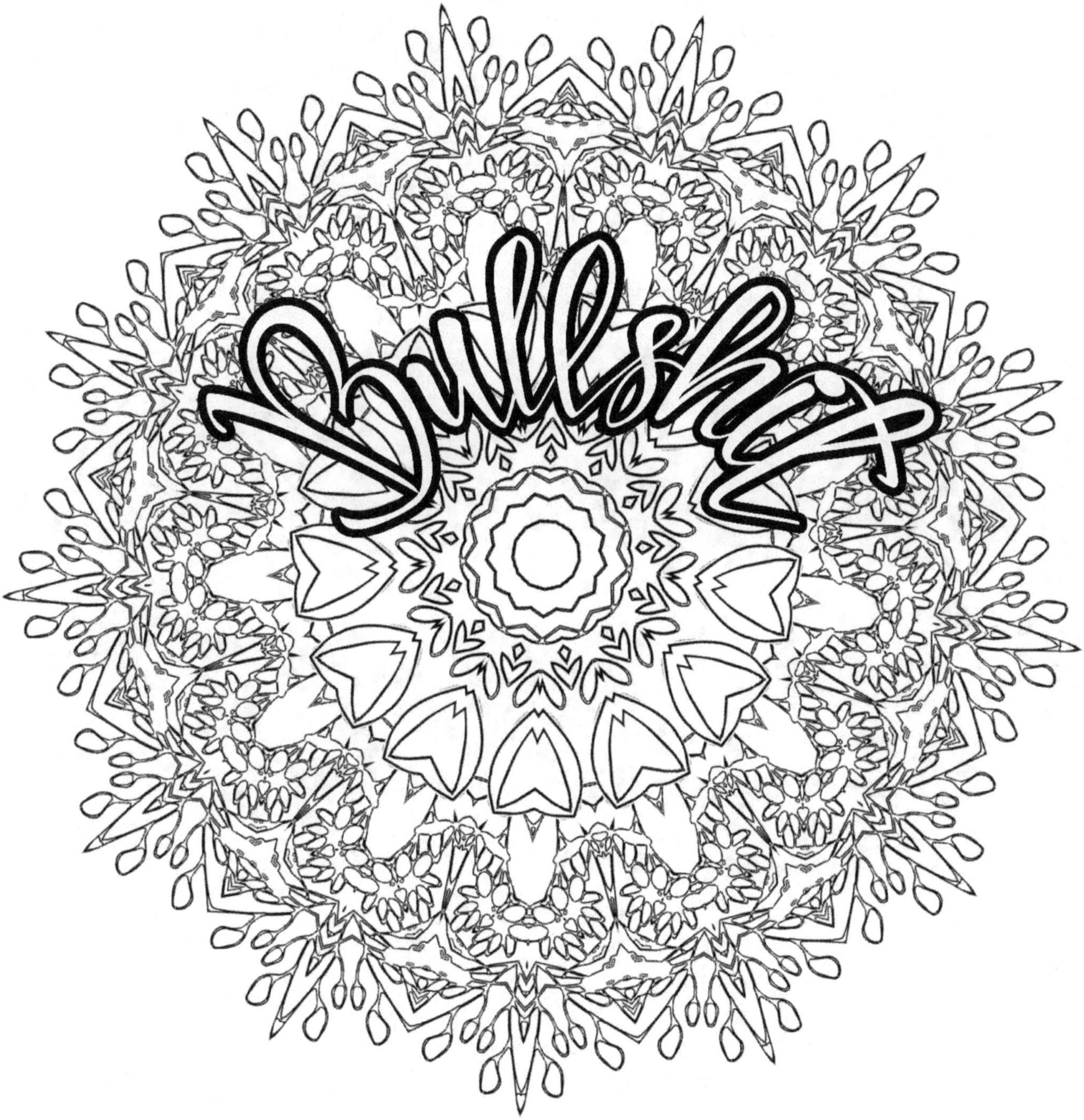
Bullshit

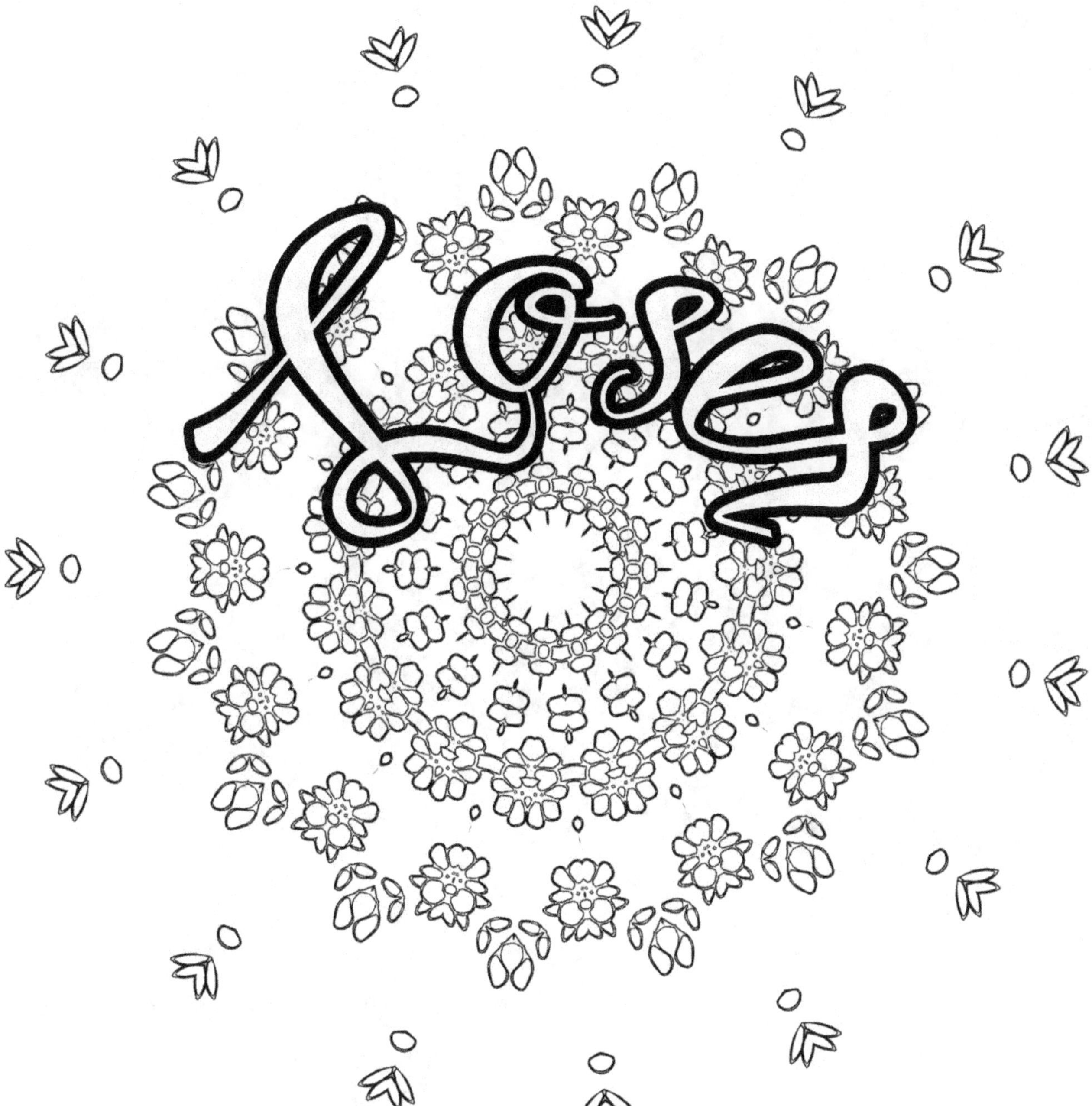
Loser

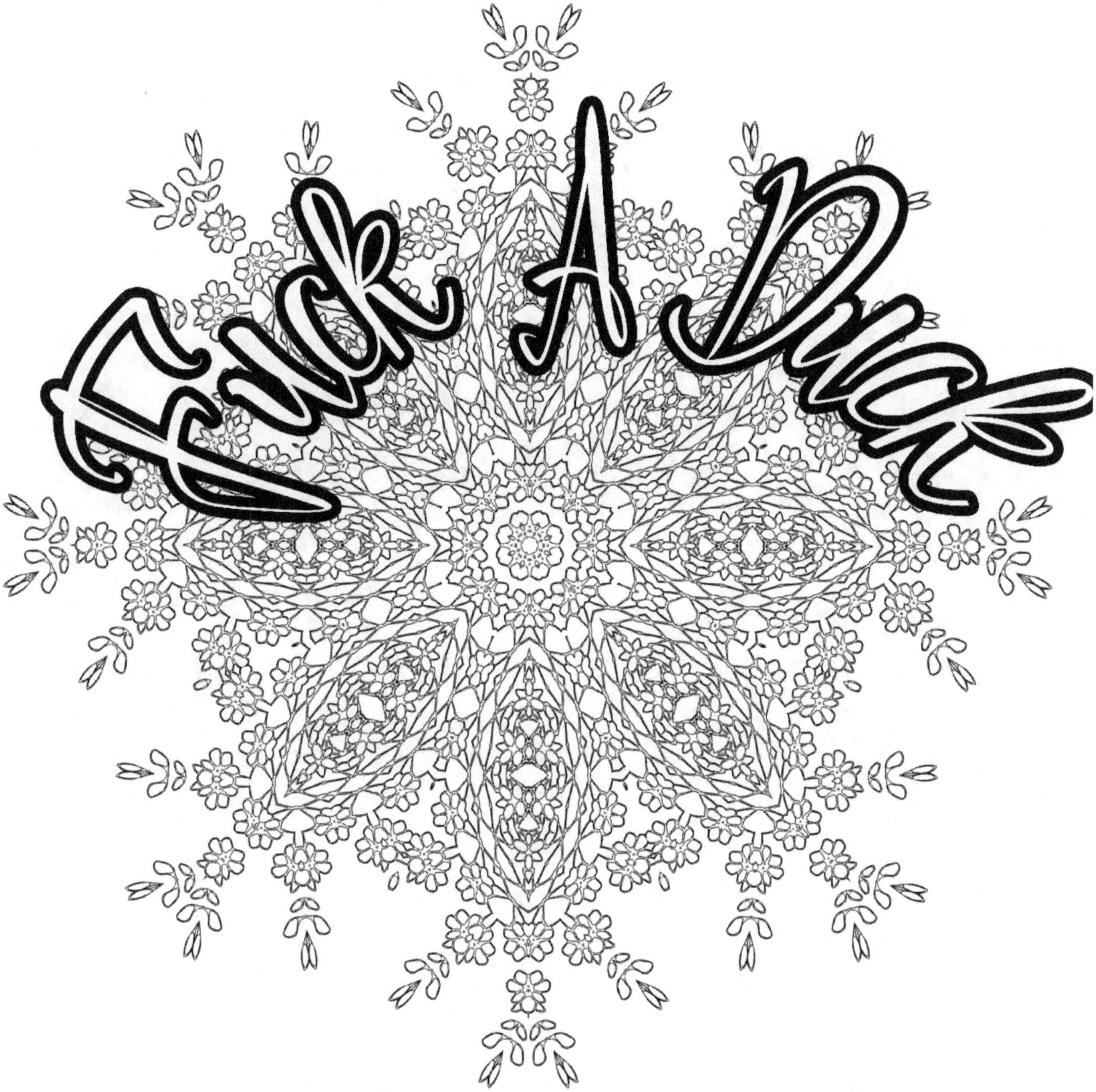
Fuck A Duck

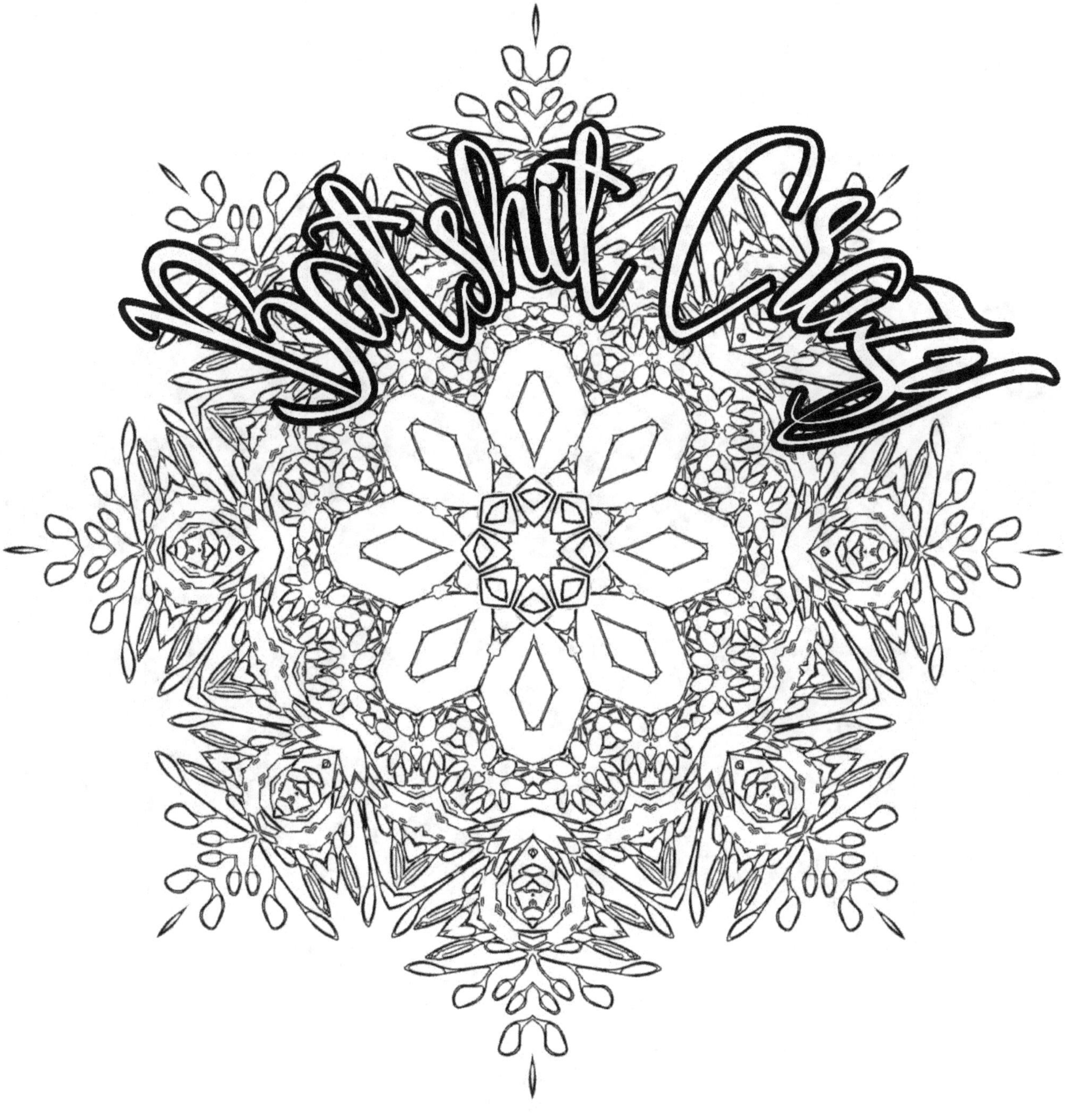
Batshit Crazy

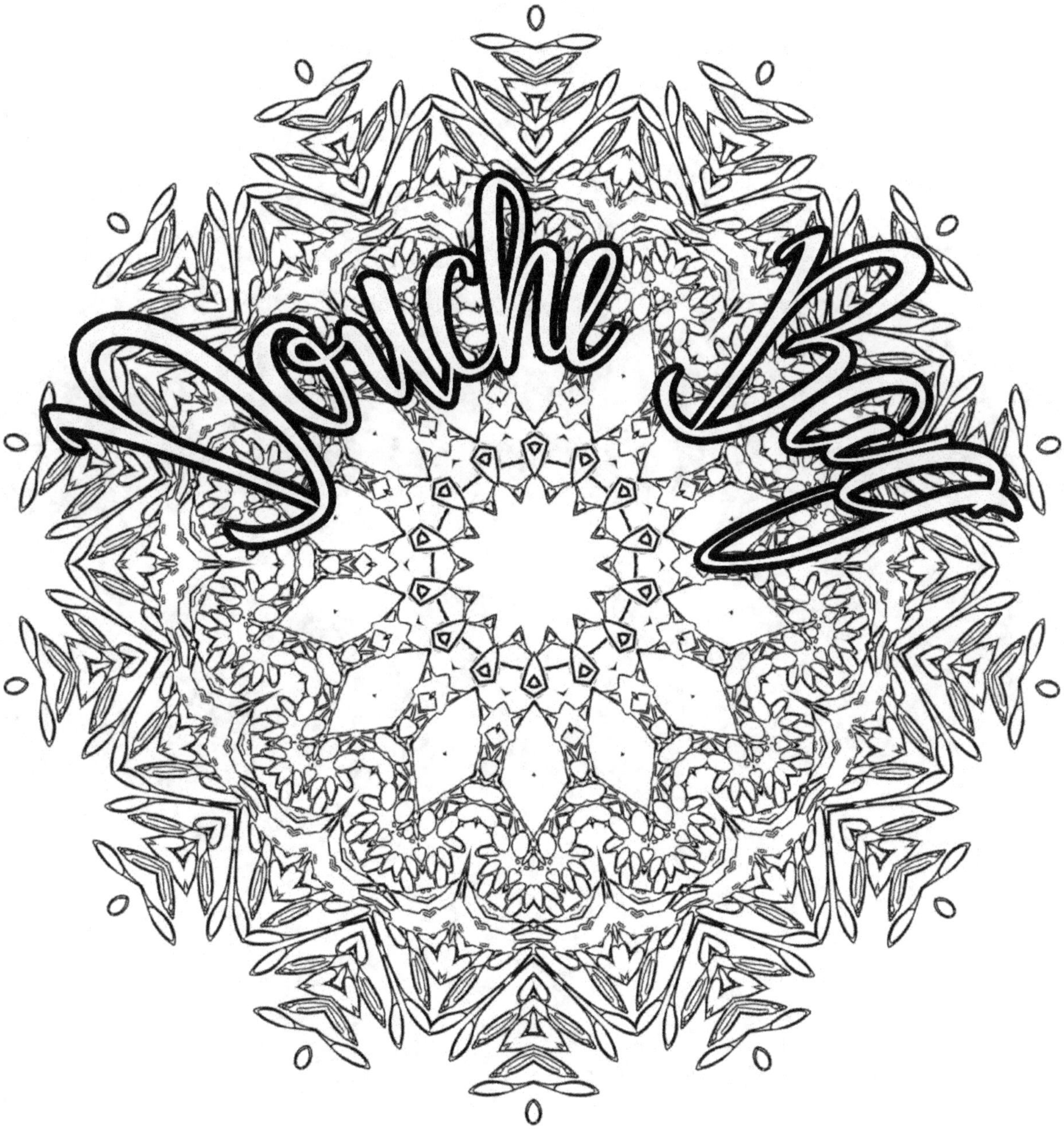
Douche Bag

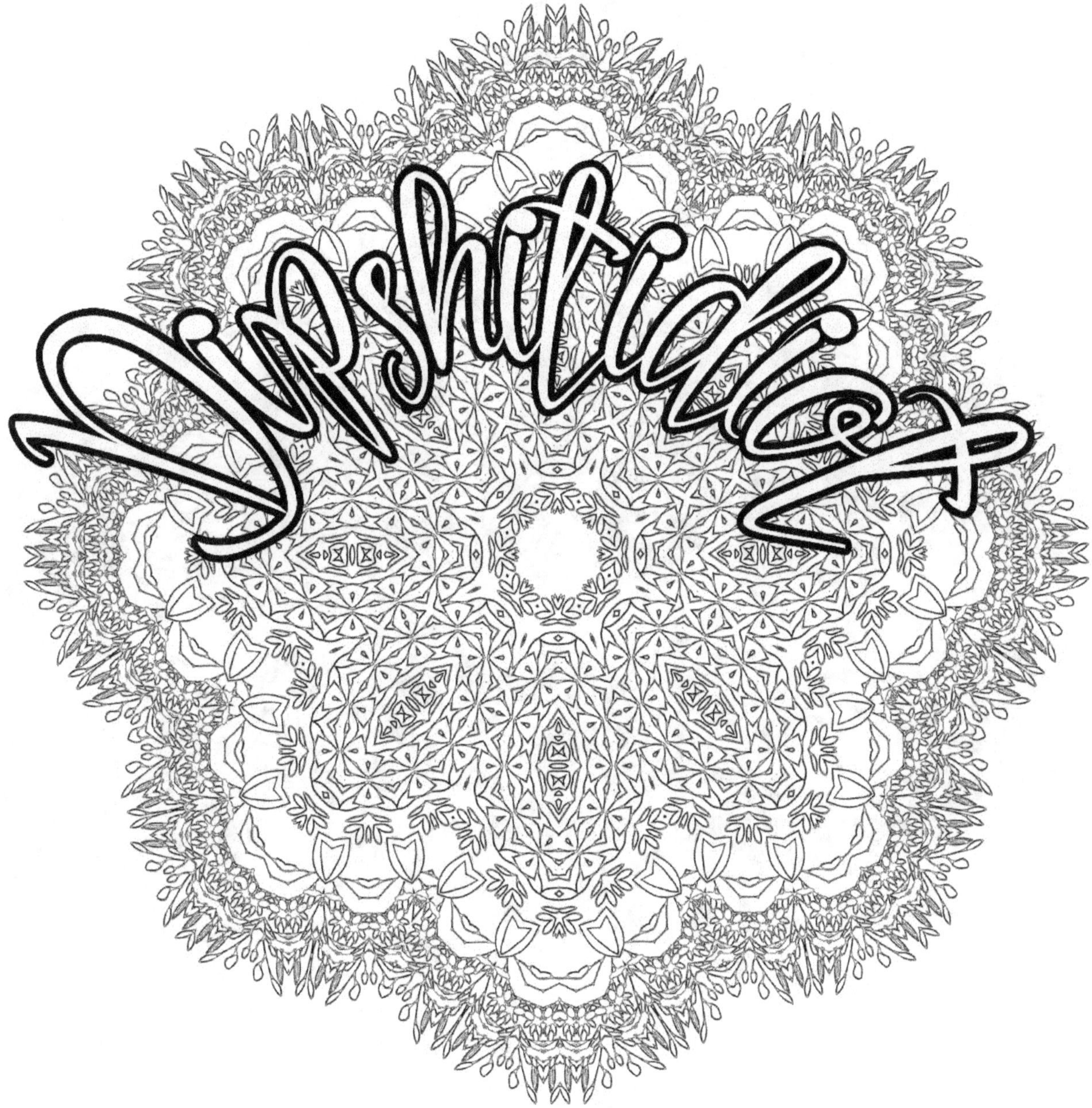
Dipshitidiot

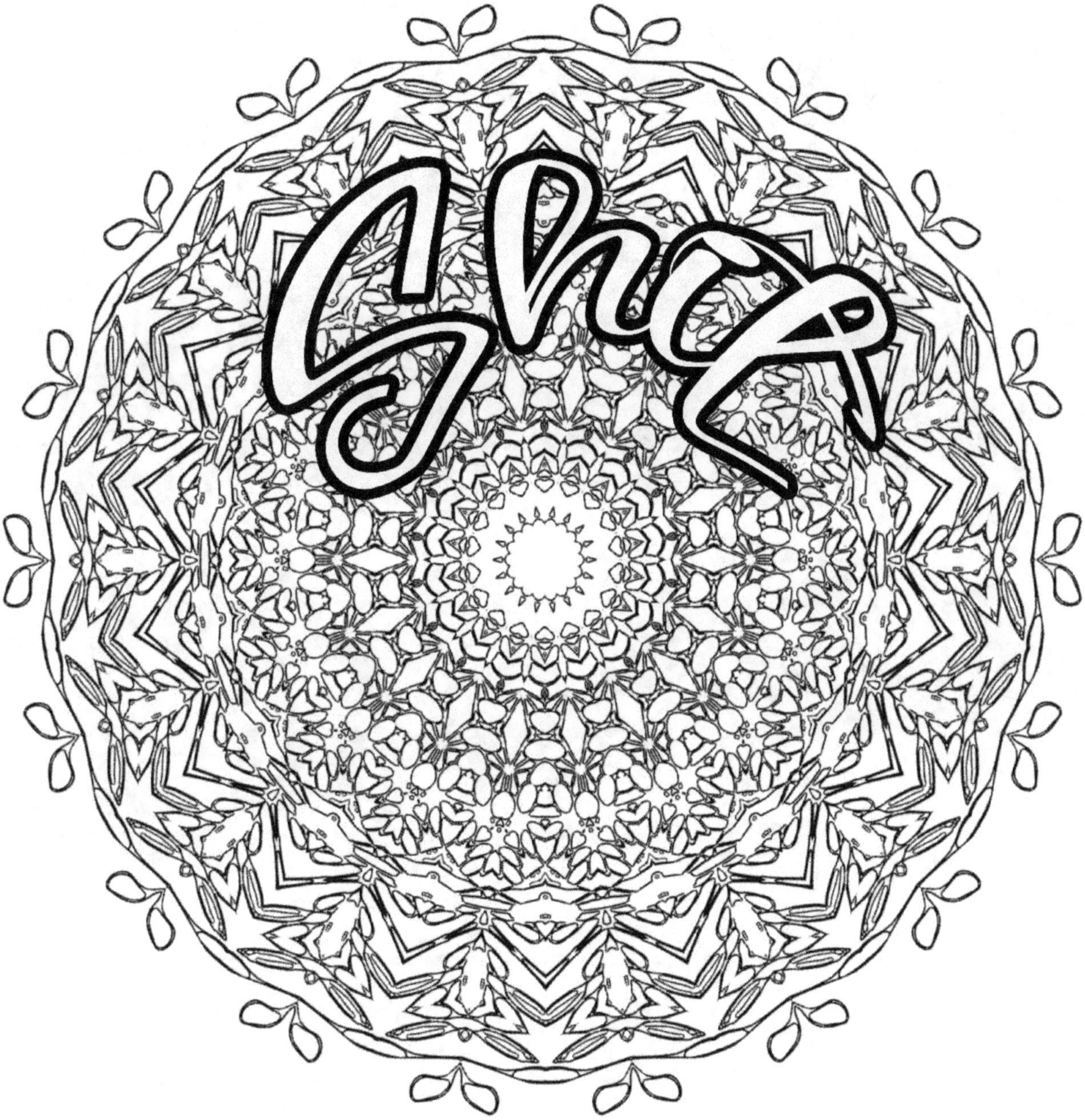
Shit

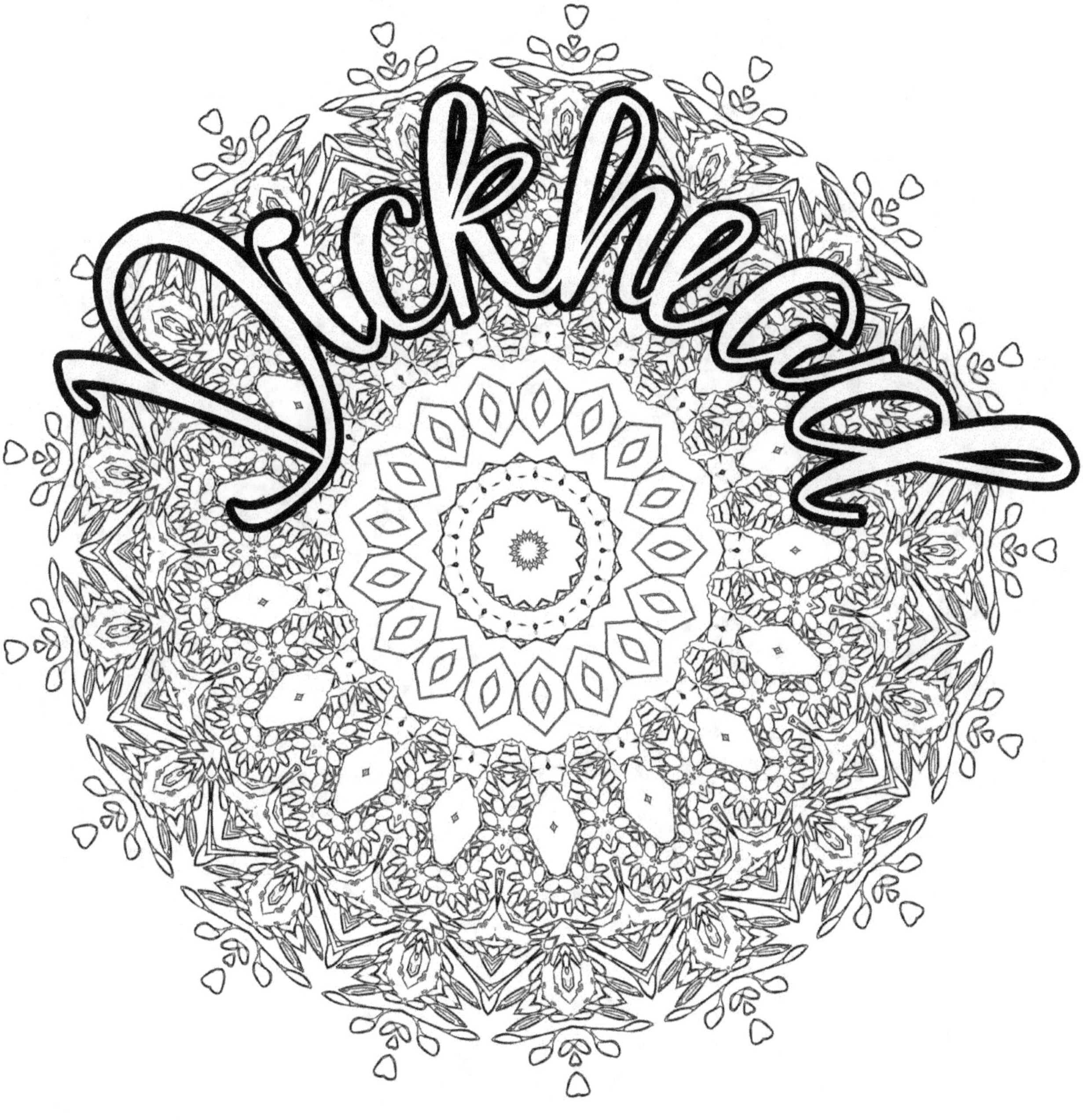
Dickhead

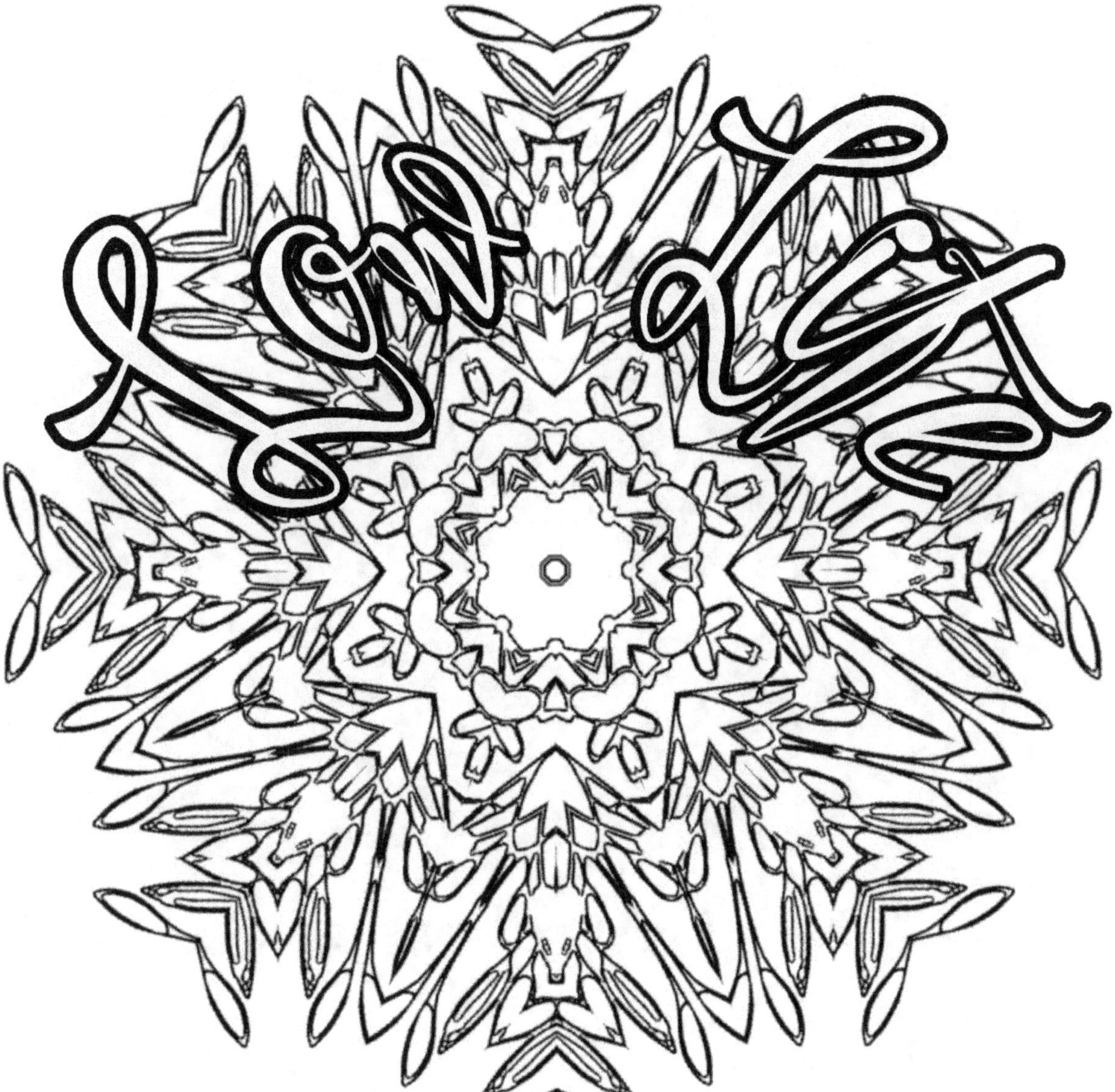
Love Life

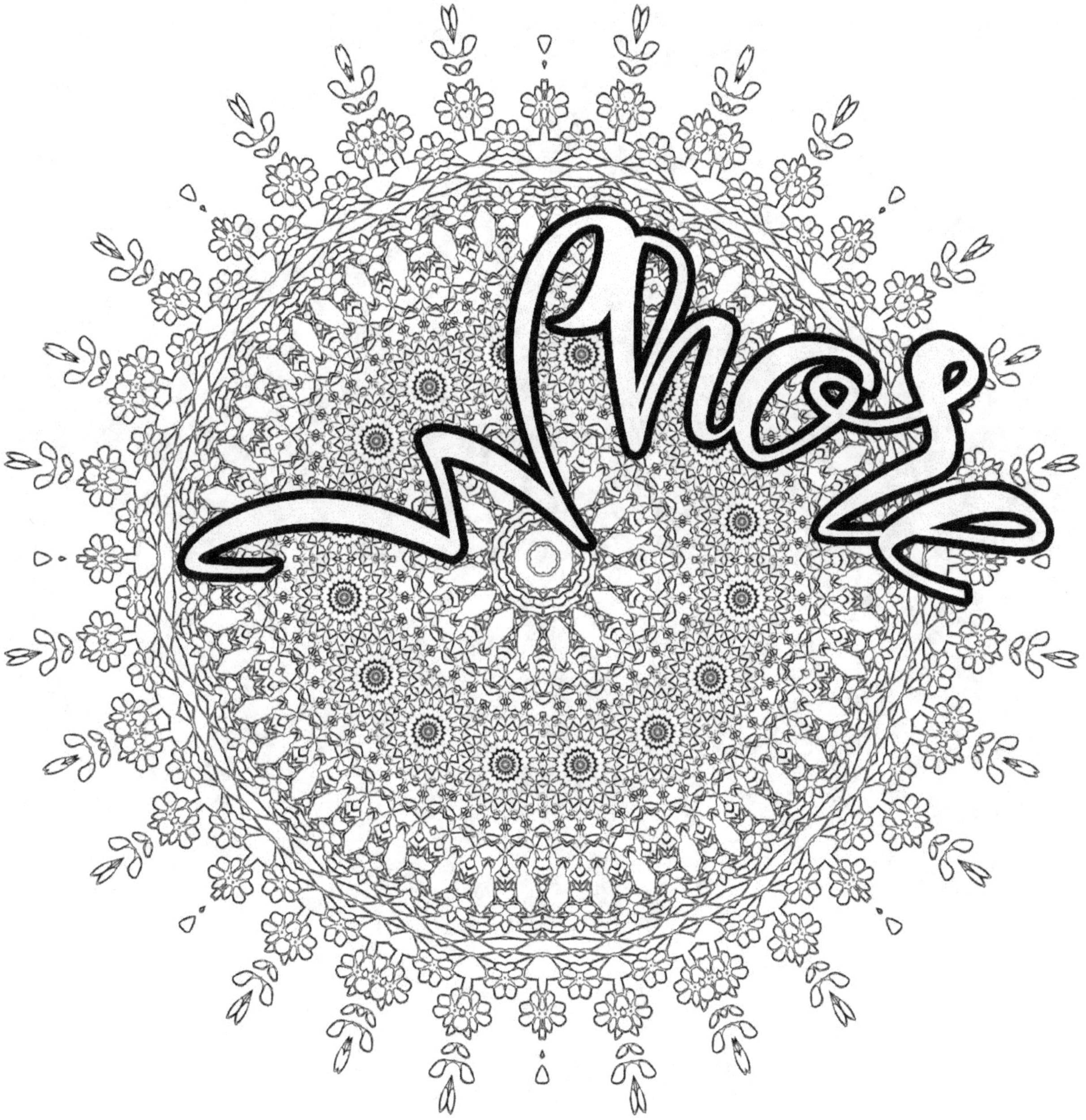
Whoa

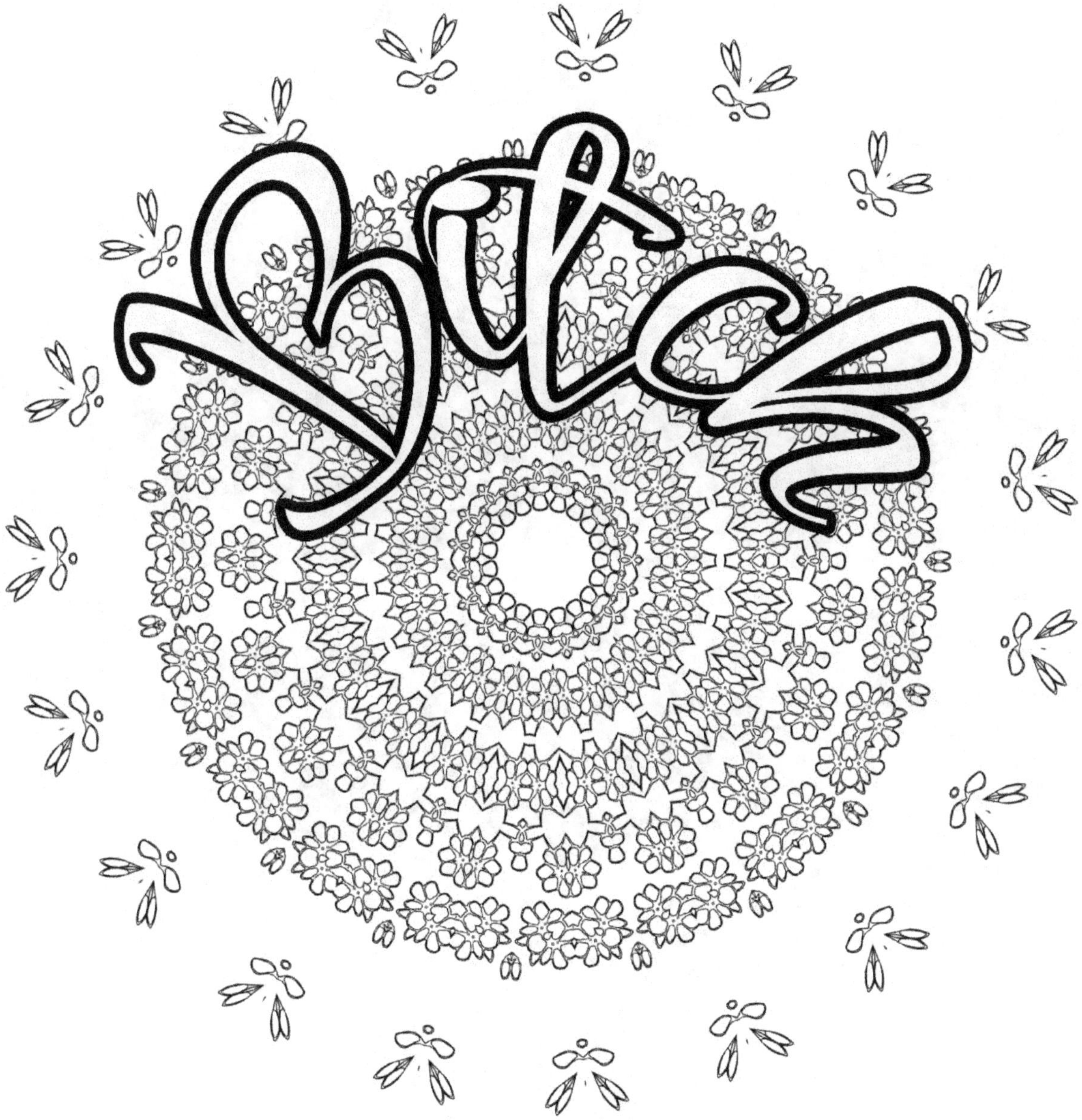
Bitch

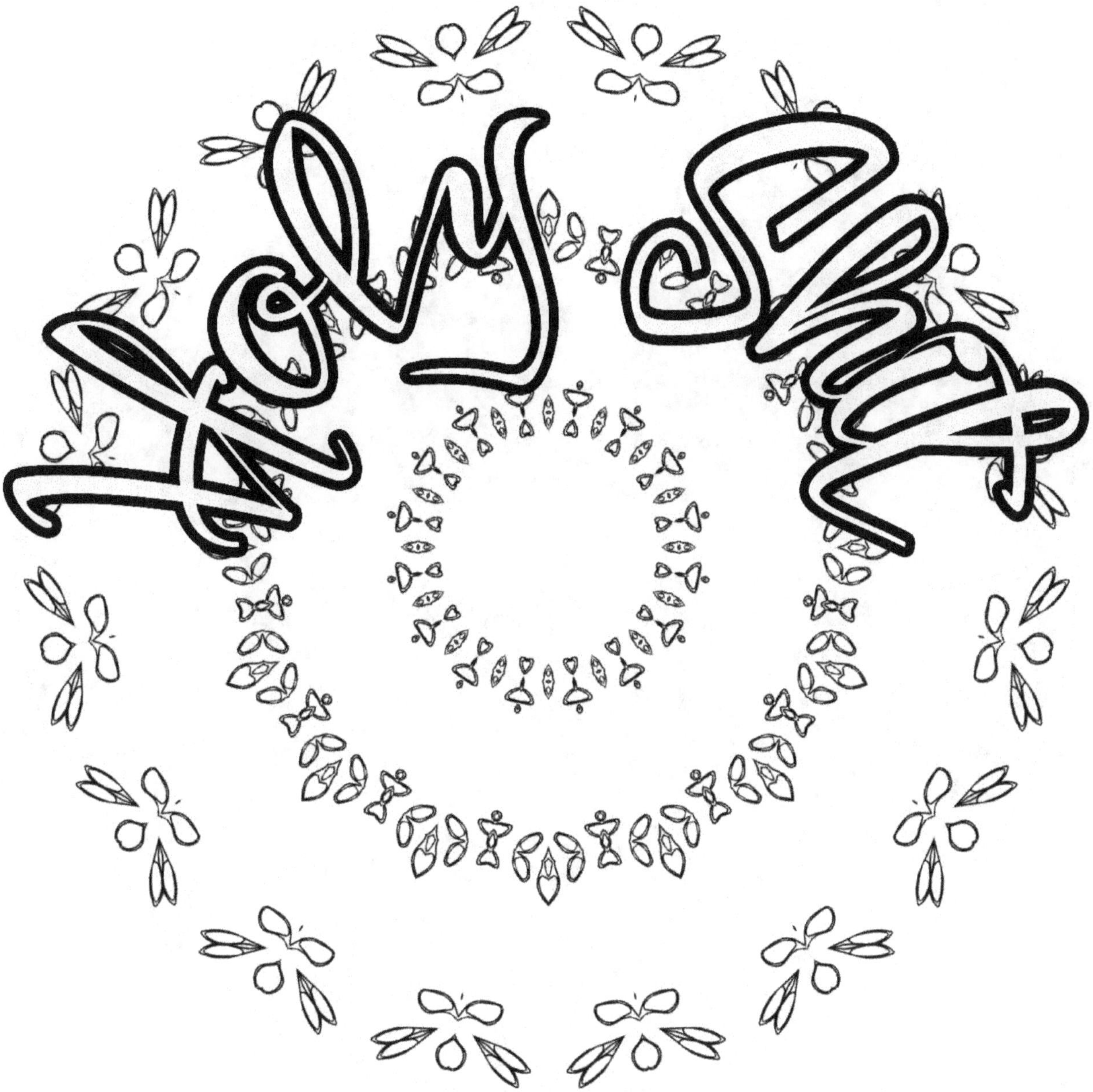
Holy Shit

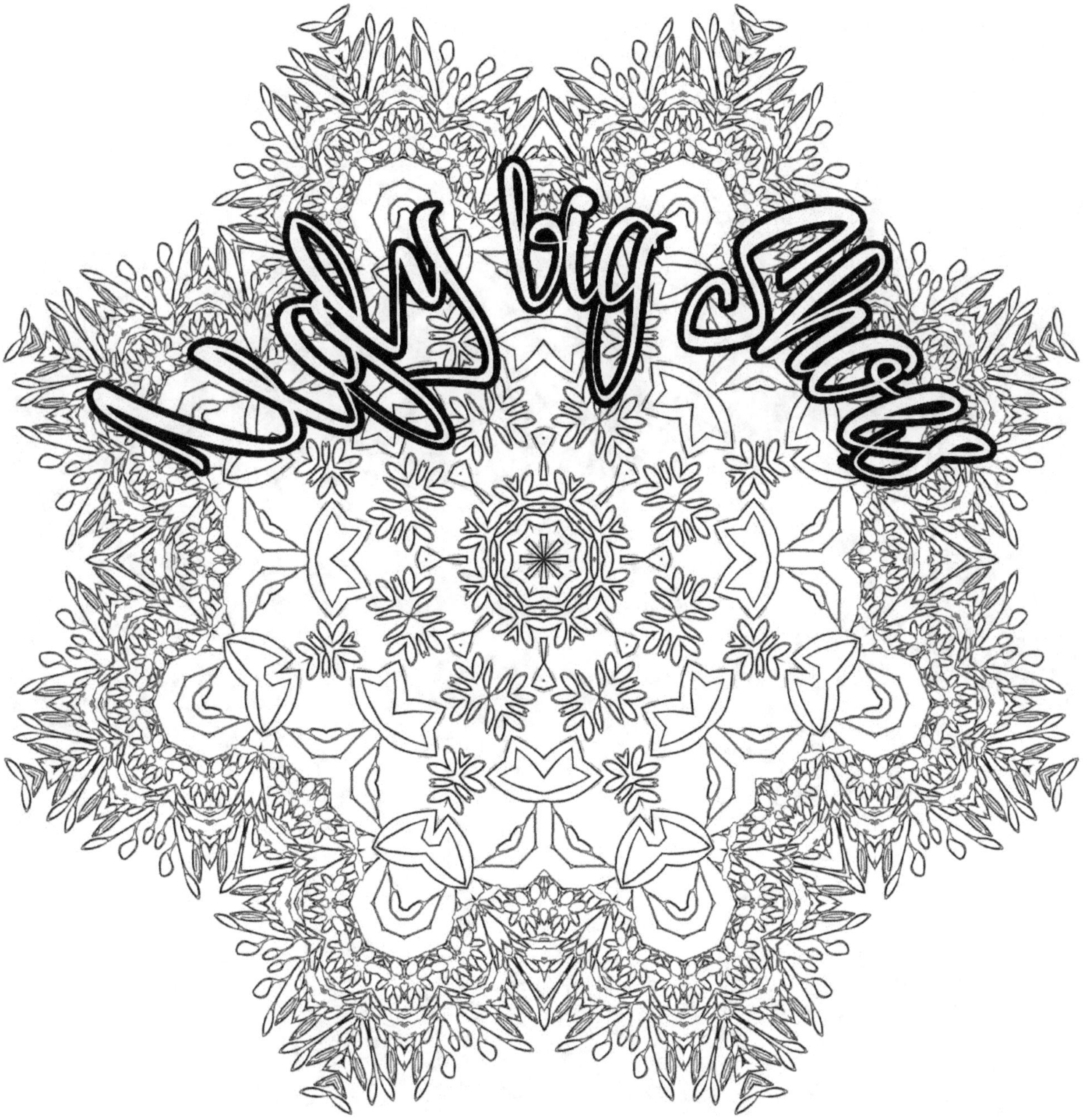
Ugly big Shoes

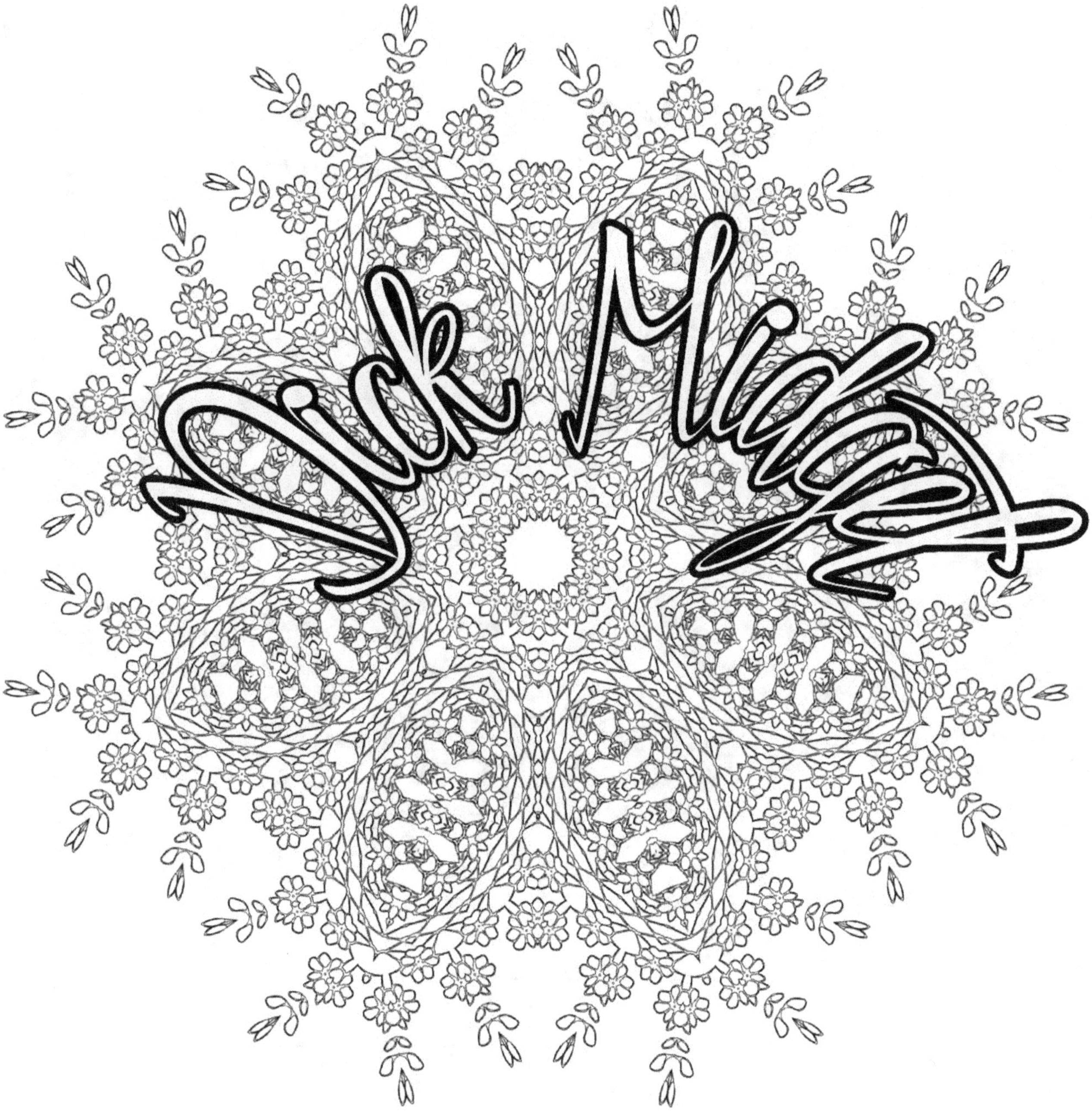
Dick Midget

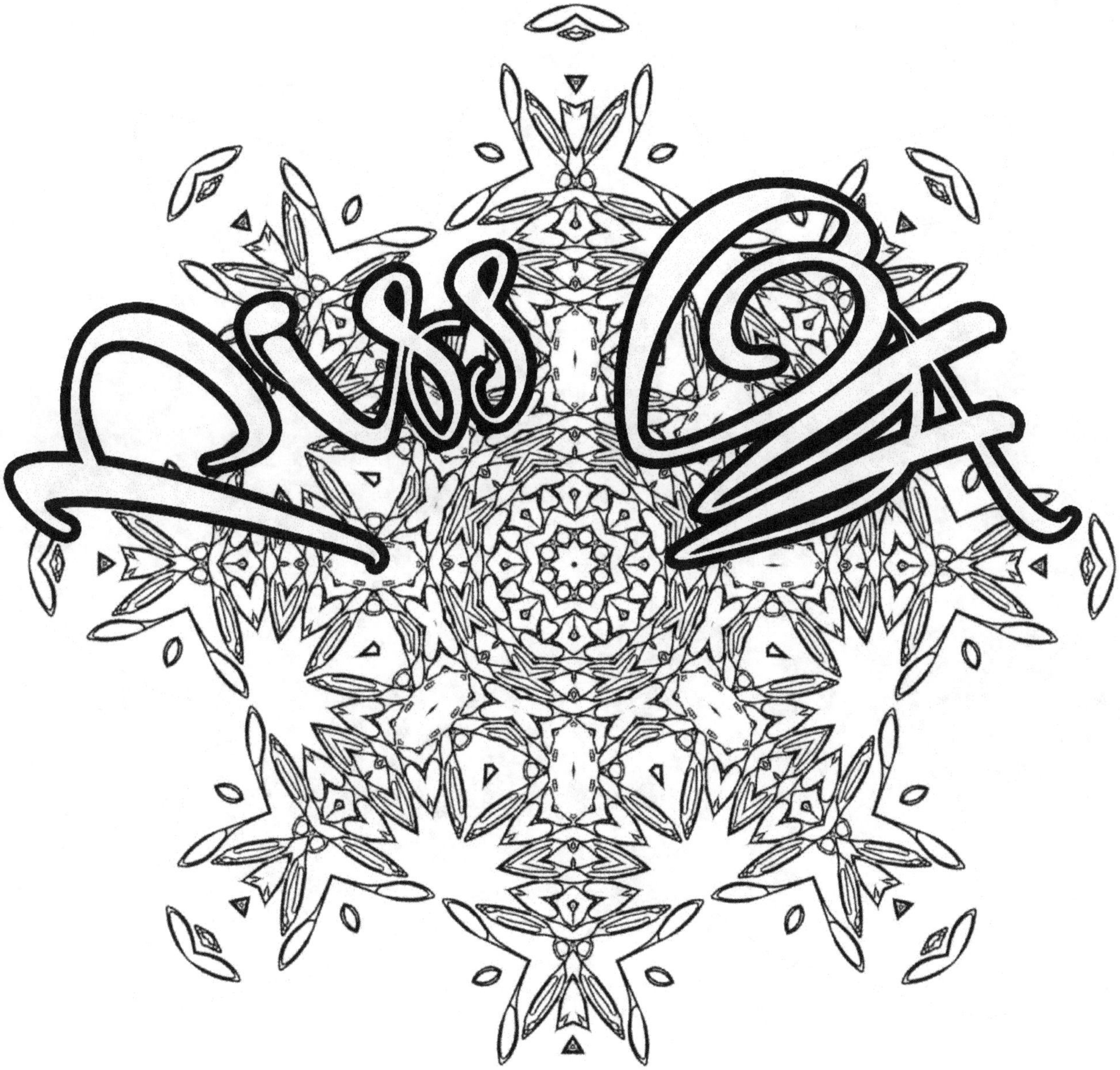
Kiss

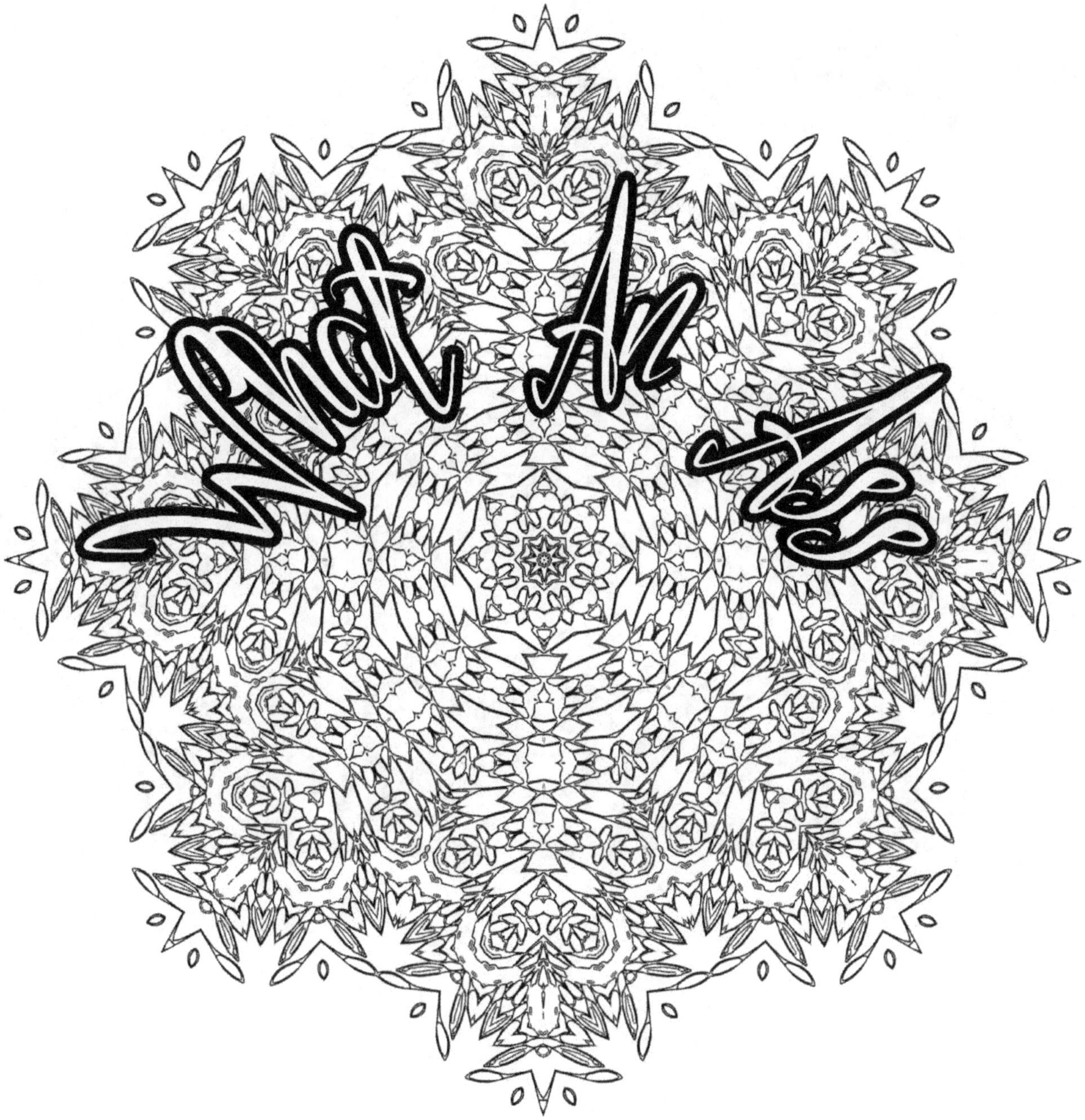
What An Ass

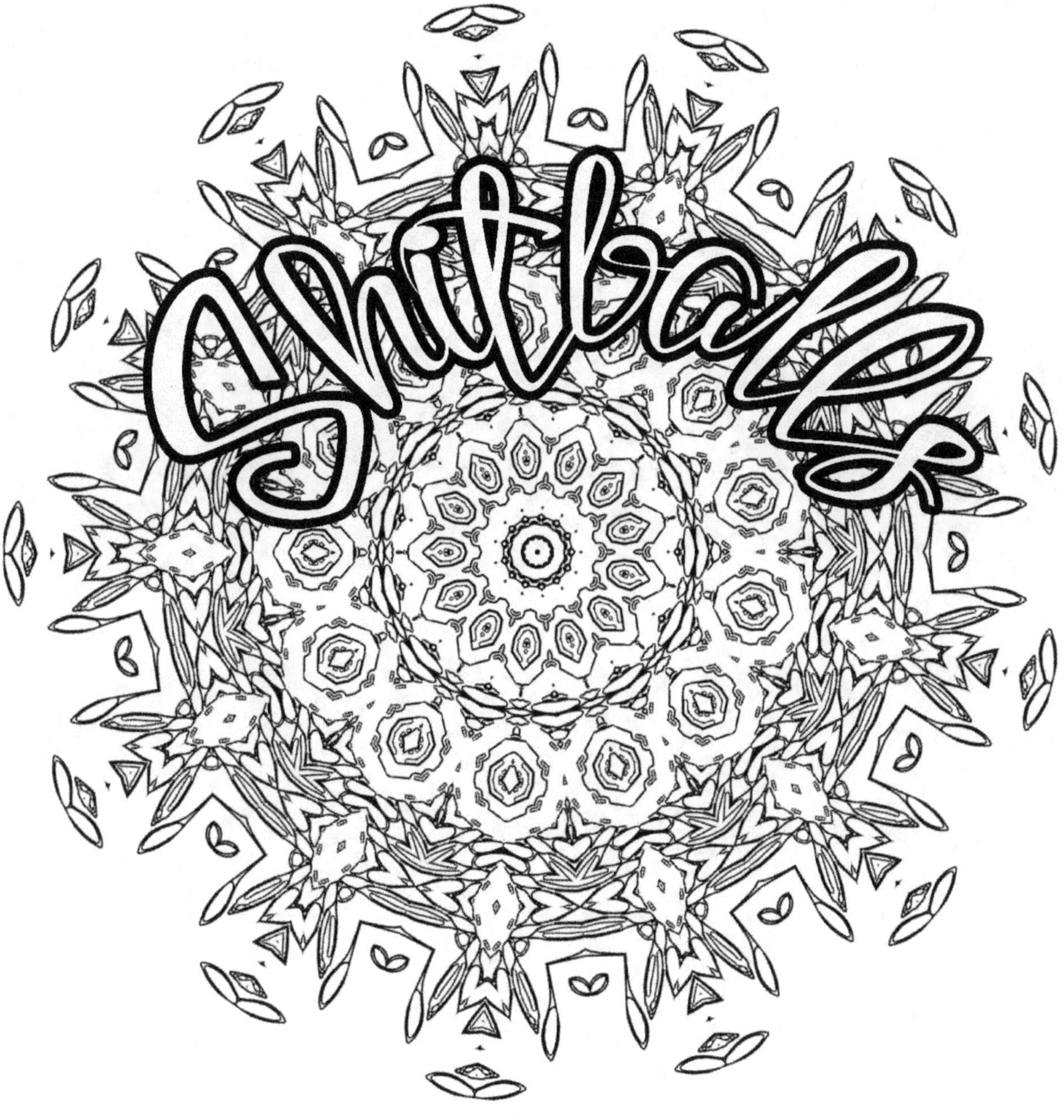
Shitballs

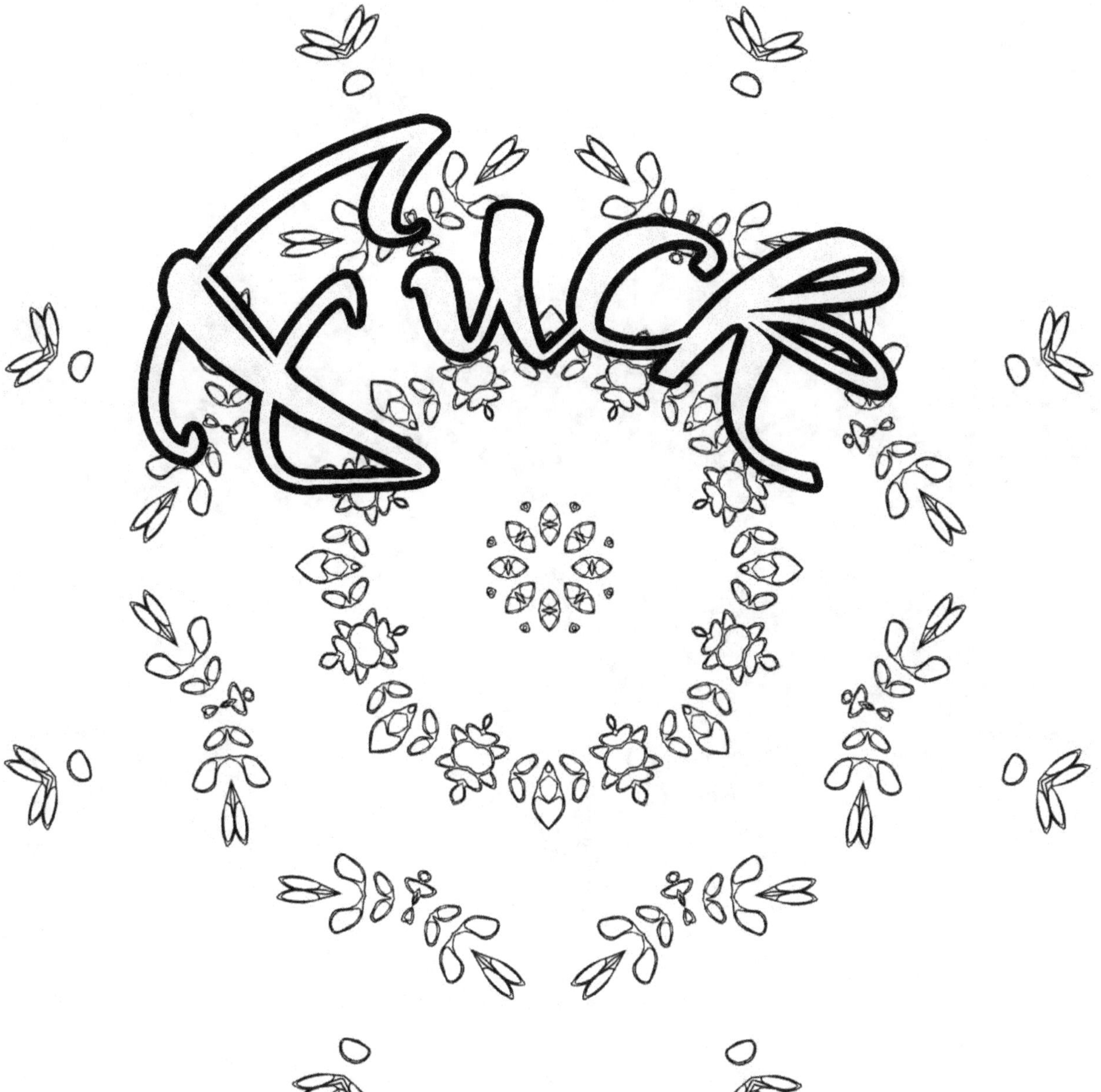
Fuck

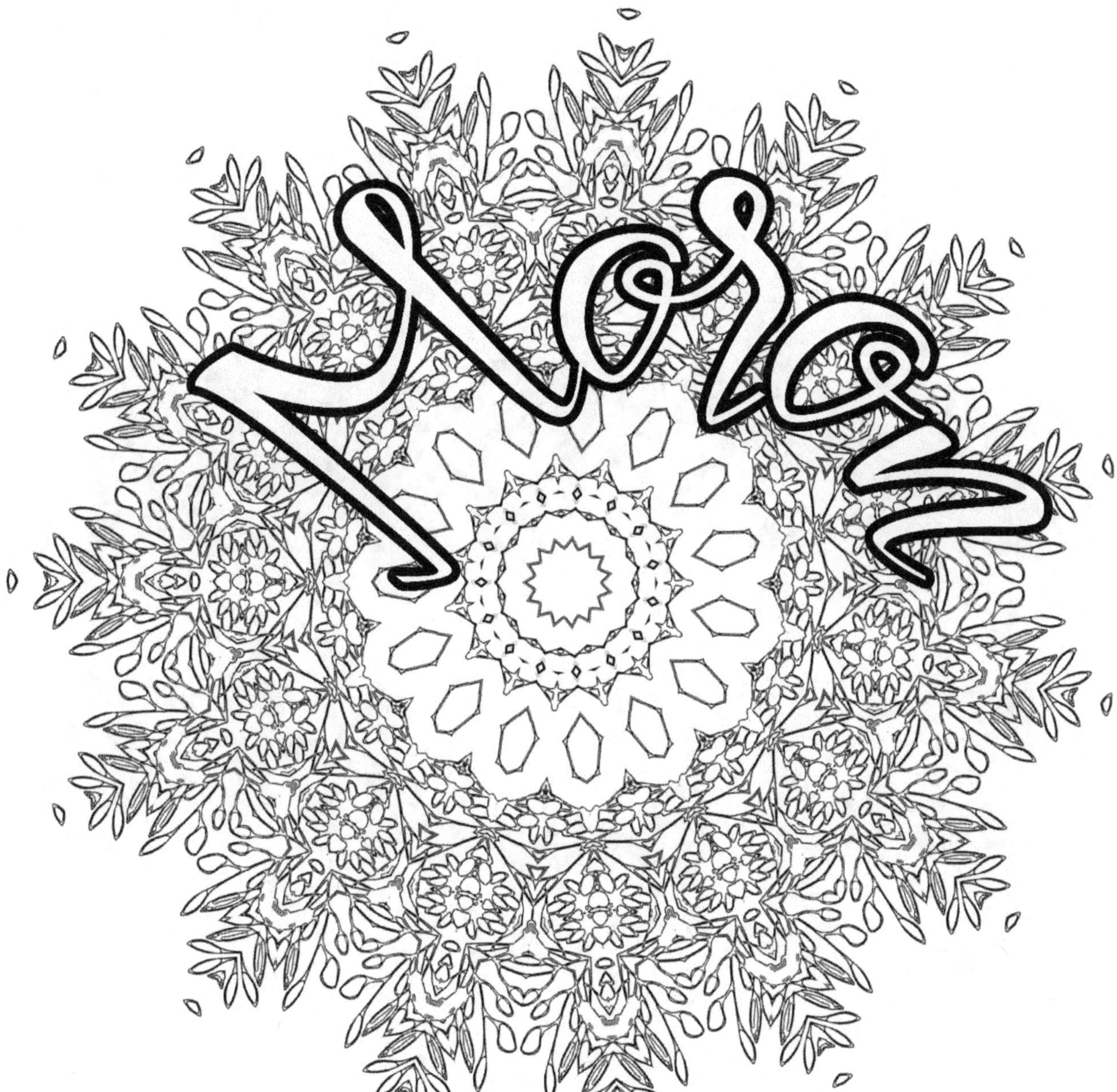

www.ingramcontent.com/pod-product-compliance
Lightning Source LLC
Chambersburg PA
CBHW081130180526
45170CB00008B/3059
* 9 7 8 1 5 4 4 6 3 5 9 9 6 *